NOAH
the story of the Ark

© 1984 Rourke Publications, Inc.

Published by Geoffrey Butcher 1983

Published by Rourke Publications, Inc., P.O. Box 3328, Vero Beach, Florida 32964. Copyright © 1984 by Rourke Publications, Inc. All copyrights reserved. No part of this book may be reproduced in any form without written permission from the publisher. Printed in the United States of America.

Library of Congress Cataloging in Publication Data

Butcher, Geoffrey.
  Noah : the story of the Ark.

  (A Little Shepherd Book)
  Summary: Tells how God spoke to Noah, telling him to build a large boat and take upon it two of every kind of animal, to save them from the great flood.
    1. Noah (Biblical figure)—Juvenile literature.
2. Noah's ark—Juvenile literature.   3. Deluge—Juvenile literature.   4. Bible. O.T.—Biography—Juvenile literature.   [1. Noah (Biblical figure)
2. Noah's ark.   3. Bible stories—O.T.]   I. Title.
II. Series.
BS580.N6B87   1984   222'.1109505   83-23058
ISBN 0-86625-248-7 (pbk.)

NOAH
the story of the Ark

Written and illustrated by
GEOFFREY BUTCHER

Rourke Publications, Inc.
A Little Shepherd Book
Vero Beach, FL 32964

Noah was a good and honest man.

He had three sons, Shem, Ham and Japhet.

God was angry with the bad people of the world.

He told Noah to build a big boat called the Ark.

God told Noah how big to build the Ark.

Noah and his sons set to work to build the Ark.

They cut down trees and sawed and hammered.

When they were finished the Ark was very big.

God then told Noah to take into the Ark two of every kind of animal.

They took animals that lived on farms.

They took animals that lived in the wild.

They took every kind of bird, animal and insect.

When the animals were safely on the Ark God spoke to Noah.

He told Noah to gather every type of food for his family and the animals.

God told Noah to board the Ark with his wife, sons and their wives.

God made the rain start to fall.

For forty days and forty nights the rain fell without stopping.

The Ark floated on the flood.

All the wicked people were washed from the earth.

Only Noah, his family and the animals were still alive on the Ark.

After one hundred and fifty days Noah sent out a dove to find land.

The dove could find no land and came back to the Ark.

A week passed and Noah sent the dove again.

This time it came back with an olive branch. It had found land.

The water went down. The Ark
came to rest on the top of
a mountain.

Noah set the animals free and thanked God for the safety of his family.

As a sign that He would
never send another flood
God created
the rainbow.

Questions to help you understand

1. What was the big boat called that Noah built?
2. What did God tell Noah to take into the Ark?
3. How long did it rain?
4. How did Noah know that the dove had found land?